CAUGHT READING

Teacher's Manual

Program Consultant
Teri Swanson, Ph.D.
Sweetwater Union High School District
San Diego, California

PEARSON

Teacher Reviewers: Colleen Arnold, Special Educator, Morningside Elementary School, Atlanta, Georgia; Robert Fass, Reading Resource Room Teacher, Martin Luther King, Jr. Junior High School, North Sacramento, California; Kathryn Mackie, Special Educator, Riverside Middle School, Dearborn Heights, Michigan; Ray Pedraza, ESL Teacher, Southwest Middle School, Reading, Pennsylvania.

Getting Ready **Program Consultant:** Teri Swanson, Ph.D.

Dr. Teri Swanson holds a Ph.D. from Wichita State University, Kansas. Her area of expertise includes the effect of phonemic awareness on literacy acquisition. She has been a speech pathologist for the past 27 years. Since 1987, she has also been in charge of reading programs for students with phonemic awareness deficiencies in the Sweetwater School District in San Diego, California.

Photo Credits: Cover images (left to right, top to bottom) © Photodisc/Getty Images, © Photodisc/Getty Images, © Photodisc/Getty Images, © PhotoAlto, © Ingram Publishing, © Photodisc/Getty Images, © Photodisc/Getty Images, © Ingram Publishing.

Note: Every effort has been made to locate the copyright owner of material reproduced in this component. Omissions brought to our attention will be corrected in subsequent editions.

Staff Credits: Joshua Adams, Melania Benzinger, Karen Blonigen, Laura Chadwick, Andreea Cimoca, Katie Colón, Nancy Condon, Barbara Drewlo, Kerry Dunn, Marti Erding, Sara Freund, Daren Hastings, Ruby Hogen-Chin, Mariann Johanneck, Julie Johnston, Mary Kaye Kuzma, Mary Lukkonen, Carrie O'Connor, Carol Nelson, Marie Schaefle, Julie Theisen, Chris Tures, Mike Vineski, Charmaine Whitman, Sue Will

ISBN-13: 978-0-7854-6648-2
ISBN-10:   0-7854-6648-7
1 2 3 4 5 6 7 8 9 10 12 11 10 09 08

1-800-992-0244
www.pearsonschool.com

CONTENTS

CAUGHT READING

Finally ... a complete, balanced solution for teaching older students to read!

Pearson's highly successful reading program, *Caught Reading*, is a comprehensive developmental reading program that takes students from pre-literacy to a fourth-grade reading level. Beginning with the prereading Worktext (*Getting Ready*), students learn new skills through each level of the program. Regardless of their reading levels, the *Caught Reading* program can help students improve their reading skills.

From Basic Literacy to Developmental Reading Instruction

Caught Reading Teacher's Manual

The *Caught Reading* program includes a prereading Worktext (*Getting Ready*) followed by seven levels of reading instruction. The Teacher's Manual provides an easy-to-follow instructional plan with the following features:

- Phonemic awareness

- The alphabetic principle and basic phonics

- Explicit phonics, decoding, and word attack skills

- Fluency, reading comprehension, and literary analysis instruction and practice

- Integration of all four language skills (reading, writing, speaking, and listening)

- Spelling in every skill-based lesson

- Prereading and postreading activities for the novels

- Opportunities for independent reading

- Connections to classic literature

- Comprehensive placement and assessment

- Extensive reteaching suggestions

Getting Ready Worktext

The *Getting Ready* Worktext helps students learn and practice the basics of reading in an appealing yet mature context and includes:

- Brief, lively reading selections

- Exposure to a wide variety of reading genres

- Engaging reading-based activities

Caught Reading Worktexts 1–7

The Worktexts provide opportunities for students to develop skills and apply them to reading selections throughout each of the seven levels. Each Practice Lesson gives students the chance to practice and extend their reading and writing skills.

- Word attack skills

- Comprehension and analysis skills

- Cooperative learning activities

- Opportunities to develop writing skills

- Emphasis on basic reading skills

- Cross-curricular connections in Levels 4–7

Reading Levels

Getting Ready	basic literacy	Worktext 4	2.5
Worktext 1	beginning	Worktext 5	3
Worktext 2	1.7	Worktext 6	3.5
Worktext 3	2.1	Worktext 7	4

Sustained Reading at Every Level

Midway Novels

These novels are taught at the midway point of each level of the program. The content is age-appropriate and vocabulary is completely controlled. These novels:

- Reinforce learned vocabulary
- Apply phonics skills
- Focus students on reading for meaning
- Provide a successful reading experience to build students' confidence

Final Novels

Additional novels at the end of each level of the program provide more sustained reading for students. These novels:

- Contain controlled vocabulary and decodable words
- Capture the interest of middle and high school students
- Provide an engaging and successful reading experience

Assessment for Every Level

Caught Reading Assessment Manual

The *Assessment Manual* consists of placement tests to determine the appropriate level of placement for each student and two comprehensive assessments per level to measure each student's progress. You can also use the *Manual* to help diagnose gaps in your students' reading skills.

- Additional practice of phonics skills
- More opportunities to develop fluency
- Reading comprehension
- Opportunities to practice writing
- Review of Worktext stories and concepts

Literature Connection

The *Pacemaker*™ *Classics* are softcover texts skillfully adapted to third- and fourth-grade reading levels. There are word-for-word read-along audiocassettes performed by professional actors available for most titles. Suggestions for thematically linking these books to lessons occur throughout the *Caught Reading Teacher's Manual.*

These Literature Connections:

* Expose students to immortal tales of classic literature

* Develop students' cultural literacy

* Help students develop literary analysis skills

* Encourage a love of literature

Extend Students' Reading With Other Pearson Products!

Pearson provides many opportunities to extend the *Caught Reading* program by incorporating classic literature and high-interest readers into the instruction, adapted to the reading level of your students.

Independent Reading Connection

The *Caught Reading Teacher's Manual* also references opportunities for independent reading. Pearson's list of high-interest readers:

* Provides a print-rich classroom environment

* Exposes students to a wide variety of genres

* Provides content-area reading

* Fosters an enthusiasm for reading

For further details see pages ix-xvii of this *Teacher's Manual.*

Program Plan

	Getting Ready	1	2	3	4	5	6	7
READING								
Phonemic Awareness								
alphabetic principle	✓							
syllabification	✓							
substitutions and deletions	✓							
blending	✓							
Phonics (Basic)								
letter recognition	✓							
initial, final, and medial consonants	✓							
long and short vowels	✓							
Phonics (Decoding and Word Recognition)								
diphthongs	✓	✓	✓					
vowel digraphs	✓		✓	✓	✓	✓	✓	✓
r-controlled vowels	✓		✓		✓		✓	
compounds		✓	✓	✓	✓	✓	✓	✓
inflectional forms		✓	✓	✓	✓	✓	✓	✓
common word families		✓	✓	✓	✓	✓	✓	✓
plurals		✓	✓	✓	✓	✓	✓	✓
possessives, apostrophes			✓	✓	✓	✓	✓	✓
Vocabulary Development								
root words		✓	✓	✓	✓	✓	✓	
prefixes			✓	✓	✓	✓	✓	✓
suffixes			✓	✓	✓	✓	✓	✓
compounds		✓	✓	✓	✓	✓	✓	✓
context clues				✓	✓	✓	✓	✓
Spelling	✓	✓	✓	✓	✓	✓	✓	✓
Reading Comprehension								
remember details		✓	✓	✓	✓	✓	✓	✓
make predictions			✓	✓	✓	✓	✓	✓
ask and answer questions about text		✓	✓	✓	✓	✓	✓	✓
retell stories				✓	✓	✓	✓	✓
read for facts					✓	✓	✓	✓
Literary Response and Analysis								
find the main idea		✓	✓	✓	✓	✓	✓	✓
write a plot summary		✓	✓	✓	✓	✓	✓	✓
describe characters		✓	✓	✓	✓	✓	✓	✓
WRITING	✓	✓	✓	✓	✓	✓	✓	✓
LISTENING AND SPEAKING	✓	✓	✓	✓	✓	✓	✓	✓
CROSS-CURRICULAR CONNECTIONS					✓	✓	✓	✓

Welcome to the *Caught Reading* program! It provides a complete and balanced solution for teaching young adults to read. The program consists of eight levels of instruction that build from pre-literacy skills to real reading.

This *Teacher's Manual* is an easy-to-use guide, providing instruction and Answer Keys for each of the program's eight levels.

A comprehensive set of placement tests appears on pages xix–xxix of the manual. These tests assesses which level of the *Caught Reading* program is most appropriate for your students, from *Getting Ready* (the basic literacy program) through Levels 1–7.

Getting Ready

Getting Ready is designed to provide all of the basics of literacy instruction in an appropriate and engaging way for the older student. The *Getting Ready* Worktext covers:

- **phonemic awareness**
- **basic phonics**
- **the alphabetic principle**

The lesson planning material for *Getting Ready* in this *Teacher's Manual* begins with a list of broad teaching objectives. These are categorized as Phonemic Awareness, Phonics, Reading, Writing, and Speaking and Listening. The lesson plans include a variety of opportunities for informal assessment and reteaching activities. As a convenience for teachers, token cards and letter cards are provided as a separate item.

The Worktext includes engaging activities and short reading passages covering a variety of genres. The pages are designed to spark and hold students' interest.

Why Teach Phonemic Awareness?

Phonemic awareness is the understanding that words are composed of various combinations of the sounds (or phonemes) of a language. Phonemic awareness is an insight about oral language and is a necessary prerequisite for beginning reading instruction.

Recent research has shown that approximately 25 percent of all students will not develop phonemic awareness on their own through normal reading instruction. Without explicit instruction, these students are at risk for becoming poor readers. These students and, in fact, all students can benefit from explicit phonemic awareness instruction as presented here in the *Getting Ready* program.

How Does Phonemic Awareness Relate to Phonics?

Understanding that running speech can be segmented into sounds is a critical step in learning to read and write an alphabetic language. The alphabet is, in fact, a code that assigns letters to the various phonemes of the language in a

Teacher's Manual Introduction

CHAPTER 2
Three-Sound, Short-Vowel Words

TOKEN LESSON A

OBJECTIVES
- Students will develop phonemic awareness by segmenting short-vowel nonsense words using tokens to represent sounds.
- Students will discriminate sounds in the initial, final, and medial positions

WORD BANK OF NONSENSE WORDS

fam	dod	lesh	tib	bev
gis	wak	bim	kem	vel
mosh	chev	thut	whit	gen
cuj	gim	tim	naz	thap
luf	daz	leth	shib	whan
rop	juv	zath	fep	roch

WORD BANK OF REAL WORDS

cap	cup	nap	not	shop
sit	fin	cut	lip	tap
sun	thin	mop	zip	
fun	map	rod	ship	

MATERIALS
Teacher's Manual, pages 7–8
Additional list of nonsense words, page 337
Token cards

▶ PHONEMIC AWARENESS

Segmenting Sounds
Place three different tokens such as a circle, triangle, and star in a row on the table in front of a small group of students.

- Say it slowly: *fam*. What is the first sound you hear in *fam*? As you say *fam*, stretch each phoneme, elongating each sound. When the first student has identified the /f/, have the student point to the first token and say /f/.

f   a   m

- Say it slowly: *fam*. What is the middle sound after /f/? Have the student say the word slowly and listen to the sound made right after saying /f/. After saying /a/, have the student point to the next token.
- Say it slowly: *fam*. What is the final sound you hear in *fam*? When the student says /m/, have him or her touch the last token. Ask the student to say the word slowly, stretching out each sound. As the student does this, point to each token. Afterward, ask the student to say it slowly and point to each token while saying each sound.
- Introduce a new nonsense word and have the next student work with another set of tokens to sound out and segment each phoneme. Repeat this routine, providing multiple opportunities for each student to work with the words found in the Word Bank.

Teacher Tip
If . . . students aren't able to identify a particular sound, *Then* . . . say the word very slowly, stretching out each sound. Be sure to say the word whole, coaching students to segment each sound by themselves.

▶ SUBSTITUTION ROUTINES

Initial Consonants
Place three new tokens in front of students, such as a circle, square, and rectangle. Demonstrate the following substitution routine.

- Say: **If this says *dod*, I'm going to make the nonsense word *fod*.** Replace the circle with a star.
- Say: **If this now says *fod*, I'm going to make *sod*.** Replace the star with a diamond.
- Say: **If this now says *sod*, I'm going to make *thod*.** Replace the diamond with a triangle.

Chapter 2 ❦ 7

LESSON 3

OBJECTIVES
- Students will apply their decoding skills by reading tongue-twister sentences that contain three-sound, short-vowel words
- Students will sort words according to their vowel sounds
- Students will decode and read a poem
- Students will write sentences that sequence the order of events in the poem

MATERIALS
Worktext, pages 14–17
Teacher's Manual, pages 15–16
Award Certificate, page 336

▶ DECODING AND READING

A. Wacky Tongue Twisters
- Read aloud the directions found on Worktext page 14. Guide students in reading each of the tongue twisters. Almost all of the words have a three-sound, short-vowel pattern. Point out any words that don't follow the pattern, such as *pickles*. When students come to this word, have them cover up *les* and decode the word *pick*. Guide them in blending both syllables together.
- When students have practiced the tongue twisters and can read them smoothly, have them use a stop watch or the second hand on the classroom clock to see how many times they can read each tongue twister in a minute.

Award a certificate to the student who not only read it the most times, but read it correctly.

B. Sort the Words
Have students read "Pal and the Pickle Pot" again. Help them begin the sorting activity by asking students to find the first short-vowel word in the tongue twister. Ask them to write it beneath the correct category. Then have students complete the activity independently.

C. Make Up Your Own Tongue Twister
Have students make up their own tongue twisters to share with classmates.

D. My Dog, Red
Have students read the poem silently. Afterward, ask them to circle any words they had difficulty sounding out. Invite students to take turns reading the poem aloud. Coach them in decoding words that are giving them difficulty.

E. What Happens First, Next, and Last?
Have students reread the poem. Taking turns, have them describe the sequence of events in their own words. On Worktext page 17, ask them to write four sentences for each stanza, ordering the events in the proper sequence.

▶ ASSESSMENT

Dictation Routine
Have students write down each sentence as you dictate it. Say the sentence a few times before having them write it. When you're ready for them to write, say each word slowly. If students are having a problem with a particular word, have them write as much of the word as they can.

1. Pat and Peg put the pet pig in a pig pen.
2. Todd will tap on the top of a tin can.
3. Sam and Sal sell shells in a shop.
4. Meg and Mack mop up the mud.
5. Biff has a bug box on his big bed.
6. We go to the set when my pet is sick.
7. I will put the mop in my van.
8. Red will sit in my lap, and I will pet him.

Chapter 2 ❦ 15

---

relatively consistent manner. Students must understand the idea behind the code (phonemic awareness) before they can begin to master it (phonics) and become literate.

Phonics instruction involves explicitly teaching the letter-sound correspondences. Learning this "code" is essential for students to begin to **decode** text (the first steps to reading) as well as **encode** text (spelling and writing).

Chapter Content

The *Getting Ready* Worktext is organized into seven chapters.

- **Chapter 1:** alphabet
- **Chapters 2–4:** three-sound words
- **Chapter 5:** four-sound words
- **Chapter 6:** five- and six-sound words
- **Chapter 7:** multisyllabic words

Consistent, Straightforward Instruction

Within each chapter, the presentation is consistent through all five lessons.

Token Lesson A The two token lessons in each chapter provide teacher-directed instruction (there is no corresponding lesson in the Worktext). Teachers use the token cards from the separate pack and a bank of nonsense words to help students develop phonemic awareness. Because tokens and nonsense words are used, students cannot rely on letter shapes or their visual memory. All nonsense words are "new" and must be decoded.

Token Lesson B In Token Lesson B, students continue to work with token cards and transition to letter cards. They begin to connect sounds to letters, developing the basic phonics skills. They also work on blending sounds. Chapters 1 and 7 do not have token lessons.

Lesson 1 Students learn spelling rules and the conventions of written English. There are accompanying activities in the Worktext for students to try out what they have learned.

Lesson 2 Students begin working with banks of real words and letter cards. They can also use the game-based activities in their Worktexts to develop and reinforce their skills.

Lesson 3 Students have an opportunity to practice their

decoding skills by reading short selections in a variety of genres. Their reading is followed by a writing exercise, where they can practice their encoding skills.

Assessment and Reteaching

- **Informal Assessments** in every chapter help track students' progress.
- **Reteaching** suggestions included in Teacher Tip boxes provide additional techniques for student success.
- **Final Assessment** helps teachers determine when students are ready to move on to *Caught Reading* Level 1.

Levels 1–7

Levels 1–7 of *Caught Reading* emphasize explicit phonics and reading skill development, as well as exposure to a wide variety of literature. Because reading skills cannot be taught in isolation, they have been integrated with writing, speaking, and listening. While Levels 1–3 of the program concentrate on developing these four language skills, Levels 4–7 also apply skills across the curriculum (Level 4—Science; Level 5—Social Studies; Level 6—Language Arts; Level 7—Life Skills).

Each of Levels 1–7 in this *Teacher's Manual* opens with an organizer.

Level Organizer
The left-hand page shows at a glance everything you will need to teach the level.

Objectives
The right-hand page lists the broad teaching objectives for the level. These are categorized as Vocabulary Development and Phonics, Reading Comprehension, Literary Analysis, Writing, and Speaking and Listening.

LEVEL 1

ORGANIZER
Level 1 of the *Caught Reading* program includes the following components:

Worktext 1

Worktext 1 includes 17 lessons, taking students from a handful of words introduced in Lesson 1 through a word list of 202 words (found on page 271 of this *Teacher's Manual*) by Lesson 17. The Practice Lessons provide students with opportunities to extend, practice, and review the content of each lesson. The Response to Reading pages allow students to practice using their new vocabulary. Tear-out Memory Chips in the back of the student book reinforce new vocabulary and can be used both independently by students and in small groups.

Midway and Final Novels 1

These novels are designed to reinforce learned vocabulary and give students the opportunity to read for meaning. Their high-interest plots encourage successful reading experiences and an appreciation for literature.

- *Hit and Run* includes only vocabulary students have learned up to the midway point of the level.
- *Crash!* includes all vocabulary learned in Level 1.

Teacher's Manual

The *Teacher's Manual* provides detailed objectives and instruction for each skill taught in the Worktext, as well as additional teaching suggestions for meaningful practice and reinforcement. The *Teacher's Manual* provides choices for flexible instruction. Comprehension questions for the Midway and Final novels are included, as well as Answer Keys for the Worktext activities and the Practice Lessons.

Assessment Manual

The *Assessment Manual* provides preassessment, ongoing assessment, and postassessment to administer to students throughout their work in *Caught Reading*. Within this Manual you will also find Midway and Final Assessments to determine the students' comprehension of the Midway and Final Novels.

66 ❧ Level 1

OBJECTIVES
Vocabulary Development

- Read a base vocabulary of words, plus additional words made up of base words and endings.
- Use the word learning sequence to remember and spell words correctly.
- Review vocabulary independently, both in and out of context, using the Memory Chips.

Phonics

- Learn to recognize words with *s*, *er*, *ing*, *'s*, *es*, *ed*, *est*, and *th* endings.
- Combine familiar words into compound words.
- Recognize the letter groups *ay*, *at*, *alk*, *all*, *an*, *ike*, *ake*, *ad*, *orp*, *ight*, and *eam* at the ends of words.
- Combine initial letter sounds and initial consonant blends with letter groups.

Reading Comprehension

- Remember details from a story.
- Identify the main idea of a story.
- Determine plot sequences.

Literary Analysis

- Identify characters, settings, and key events.
- Identify the main problem or conflict of the plot and how it is resolved.

Writing

- Write brief narratives that move through a logical sequence of events.
- Write descriptions of setting, character, objects, and events in detail.

Speaking and Listening

- Discuss issues presented in stories.
- Listen attentively as others read aloud.
- Describe plot sequences.

Every lesson is organized in an easy-to-manage format that provides thorough teaching support in a consistent manner.

Organization Box

Lessons begin with an organization box designed to make daily planning a snap. For easy reference, the **lesson objectives** are clearly listed, along with **word banks** of vocabulary presented in that lesson. Also included is a **materials list** that saves preparation time.

Reduced Worktext Pages

As an **ease-of-management** convenience, reduced Worktext pages are displayed at point-of-use.

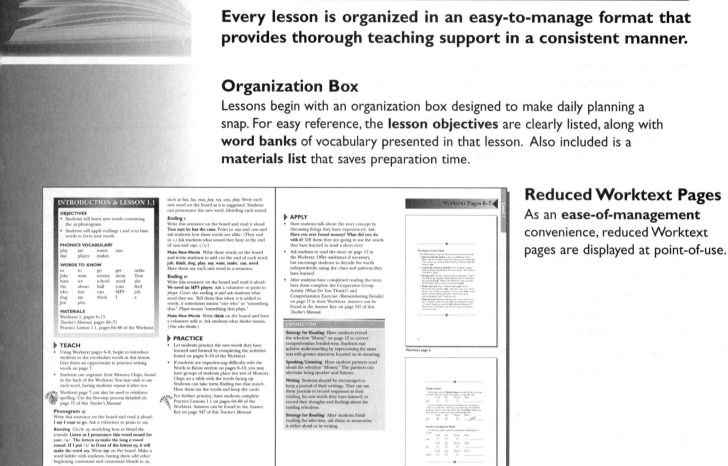

Teach, Practice, and Apply

The three-step lesson plan itself follows a clear, consistent instructional design with three basic steps: Teach, Practice, and Apply. Each lesson includes instruction in:

- **explicit phonics**
- **word-attack skills**
- **spelling and vocabulary development**
- **comprehension skills**

Connections

Because all four language skills are so closely tied together and are of little value in isolation from each other, the lessons also include suggestions and activities to help integrate **writing, speaking, and listening skills** along with the basic reading skills.

More Practice

References to the Practice Lessons in the **Worktexts** are clearly marked.

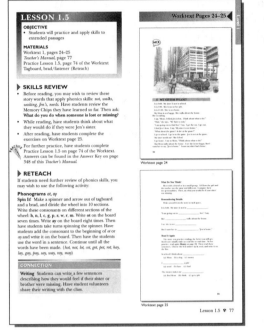

Skills Review

There are ample opportunities for **reviewing phonics skills and checking comprehension**. Throughout the levels, there are Worktext lessons that are completely free of new words and skills. In these lessons, students can read with minimal frustration and enjoy the reading experience.

Reteach

For additional direct instruction, a Reteach activity has been included. Every Reteach activity presents a skill in a new way. In this way, **all students**, regardless of their learning style, **have an opportunity to succeed.**

Midway and Final Novel Lessons

At the midway and final point of every level, special lessons are provided to give extra support for teaching the novels. These lessons include summaries of the novels, as well as prereading activities to activate students' prior knowledge and to get them involved and interested. Postreading activities with comprehension questions (answers included) are also part of the lesson instruction.

Assessment

References to the **Practice Lessons** are provided throughout each level.

Home/School Connection

These lessons provide suggestions for students to share the novels at home with family and friends.

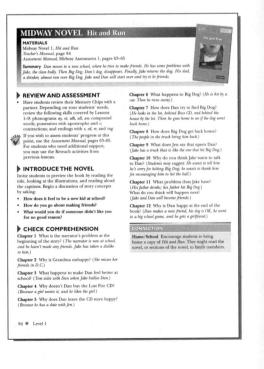

Students With Differing Learning Styles

People of all ages learn and think in different ways. Although most people receive information through their five senses, each individual tends to prefer learning through a particular sense, such as sight or sound. When educators refer to "learning styles," they are basically talking about the different ways in which students learn and think. When different learning and thinking styles are taken into account in planning lessons, teachers can help all their students understand new information and ideas.

The activities in Pearson's *Caught Reading* program can be used to address the different learning styles of students. The following ideas will help you meet the needs and preferences of every student in your class.

VISUAL LEARNERS

- Write the Phonics Vocabulary and Words to Know on the board, overhead transparency, or chart paper so students can refer to them.

- Write instructions and directions on the board. After giving instructions, put examples on the board.

- Use graphic organizers, such as word webs, tables, and charts to help students visualize the information.

- Provide a print-rich environment in your classroom.

AUDITORY LEARNERS

- Read aloud the Phonics Vocabulary and Words to Know so students can hear the words.

- Read aloud instructions and directions, and have students repeat them back to you.

- Invite student volunteers to read aloud the Worktext selections and excerpts from the novels.

- Provide time for class and small-group discussion.

- Read aloud to students every day.

TACTILE LEARNERS

- Encourage students to write the Phonics Vocabulary and Words to Know so that the movement of their hands can help them remember the words.

- Encourage students to make graphic organizers and draw pictures to illustrate content and story sequence.

- Allow students to manipulate the Memory Chips for active involvement.

Teaching English Language Learners (ESL/LEP)

Teaching English Language Learners requires good teaching techniques directed toward students' special needs. Pearson's *Caught Reading* program is particularly well suited for the English learners in your classroom. Activities that support phonics instruction, plus the integration of the four language skills—reading, writing, speaking, and listening—make the program particularly relevant to these students.

The key to language acquisition is exposure to the language in meaningful contexts. *Caught Reading* provides a variety of reading genres for your students (including short articles, story selections, plays, poetry, content-area reading, and classic literature). There are also many opportunities for meaningful practice for students, both oral and written.

Among the effective strategies, activity types, and coverage included in the *Caught Reading* program that support the teaching of English Language Learners are the following:

- Cooperative learning activities

- Pair and group work

- Four-skills coverage (reading, writing, speaking, and listening)

- Shared reading

- Exposure to reading genres and oral language registers

- *Getting Ready* (basic literacy component of *Caught Reading*)

- Built-in redundancy (repetition and reteaching)

- Age-appropriateness

- Cloze activities

In implementing English Language Learner strategies, you may consider the following additional activities, which can be easily integrated into *Caught Reading*.

- Modeling (visual or auditory examples for explaining or demonstrating what is expected)

- Building charts with information about students in the room, activities in the school, or places in the town or neighborhood, from which reading and writing can evolve

- Having a library of taped stories, such as *Pacemaker*™ *Classics* audiocassettes, an available tape player or CD player, and printed versions of the stories so that students can follow along in their books as they read

- Reading to students, having native speakers read to them, having students reread silently, and having them act out stories they have read

Literature Connection

One of the keys to reading success is exposure to a print-rich environment. Pearson provides suggestions throughout *Caught Reading* for building a classroom library. The *Pacemaker™ Classics* are adaptations of many of the literary works on state reading lists. These books inspire reading success with skillful adaptations of well-known literature and plays. Created for students reading below the fourth-grade level, each classic retains the integrity and tone of the original.

These *Pacemaker™ Classics* can be used to stimulate class discussion as well as to develop comprehension and literary analysis skills. To further enrich students' listening skills, Pearson provides read-along audiocassettes for many of the titles. Read by professional actors, these audiocassettes bring the drama of the classics to life for students.

The coordinating Study Guides for teachers provide critical background notes about the author, or playwright, and the time period. These guides help organize class discussions and literary analyses of the literature—plot summaries and character descriptions—as well as cooperative teaching activities.

The following is a list of selected *Pacemaker™ Classic* titles. Other suggestions thematically linking classics to lesson instruction are provided throughout Levels 4–7 of this *Teacher's Manual*.

Adventures of Huckleberry Finn	Jane Eyre
The Adventures of Tom Sawyer	The Last of the Mohicans
Anne Frank: The Diary of a Young Girl	Little Women
The Call of the Wild	Macbeth
A Doll's House	A Midsummer Night's Dream
Dr. Jekyll and Mr. Hyde	Moby Dick
Tales of Edgar Allan Poe	The Red Badge of Courage
Frankenstein	Robinson Crusoe
Narrative of the Life of Frederick Douglass	A Tale of Two Cities
Gulliver's Travels	The Three Musketeers
	The Time Machine
	20,000 Leagues Under the Sea

Look for the Pearson read-along audiocassettes and Study Guides to accompany many of these titles.

For a complete list of titles, consult your Pearson catalog, call 1-800-992-0244, or visit our website at www.pearsonschool.com.

The goal of any reading program is to create independent readers—students who read on their own both for information and for pleasure. One of the best ways to encourage independent reading is to build a library of motivating, exciting, and engaging books all written at a level accessible for students.

The Independent Reading Connection, which appears throughout the lesson instruction in this *Teacher's Manual*, is designed to provide suggestions for building classroom libraries. Pearson publishes a number of high-interest readers in a variety of genres, ranging from mysteries to adventure to real-life drama. The Independent Reading Connection provides references to titles that are thematically linked to instruction and are written at an appropriate reading level. Activities involving small group and pair work are also included.

The following is a list of some Pearson titles that might be of interest. Many titles are available in sets. Other suggestions can be found at point-of-use throughout this *Teacher's Manual*.

	READING LEVEL	ISBN
Reading Explorations (6 titles)	1-4	call for ordering info
SporTellers™ (8 titles)	2-3	0-822-46484-5 (set)
Freedom Fighters (5 biographies)	3-4	0-822-43219-6 (set)
BesTellers™ (40 titles)	2-4	0-822-45347-9 (set)
Uptown, Downtown (8 titles)	2-3	0-835-91149-7 (set)
Matchbook Five-Minute Thrillers (20 titles)	3	0-822-43103-3 (set)
World Myths and Legends I and II (16 titles)	3	0-822-44613-8 (set)
Worktales (10 titles)	2-3	0-822-47150-7 (set)
Hopes and Dreams (20 titles)	3	0-822-43818-6 (set)

For a complete list of titles, consult your Pearson catalog, call 1-800-992-0244, or visit our website at www.pearsonschool.com.

You may use the following **five-step process to reinforce spelling, vocabulary development, and word recognition** for students throughout this program. Encourage students to follow this process as they complete the Words to Know sections in their Worktext pages. The lesson instructions in this *Teacher's Manual* include reminders to introduce and reinforce spelling.

The five-step process outlined below appears in Worktext 1 for the students.

Step 1

Find out what the word is.

Step 2

Look carefully at the word. First look at the word as a whole. What shape does it have? Do any letters go above or below the line? Next look carefully at each letter in the word.

Step 3

Say the word out loud several times. Listen to all the sounds in the word as you say it again.

Step 4

Picture the word. Try to see each letter and the shape of the whole word. Practice looking at the word and saying it until you can get a good mental picture of it.

Step 5

Write the word.

Words to Know

Every time you see **Words to Know** you will use the five steps to learn some new words. You will see a chart like this.

	Look	Say	Picture	Write
job	☐	☐	☐	_____

As you complete each step in learning a new word, put a check (✓) in the box. When you can write the word without looking, write it on the line below the word **Write**. When you have learned a word, your chart will look like this:

	Look	Say	Picture	Write
job	☑	☑	☑	job

Practice Learning New Words

Use the five steps to practice learning the following new words.

	Look	Say	Picture	Write
dog	☐	☐	☐	_____
say	☐	☐	☐	_____
think	☐	☐	☐	_____

7

Worktext 1 page 7

PLACEMENT TESTS

The following pages include placement tests for the *Caught Reading* program that will allow you to place your students in the appropriate instructional level. Your initial assessment of each student may be administered at any level of the program to aid you in quickly identifying the appropriate instructional level for that student.

Included first is a description of the placement tests and instructions regarding administering and scoring each of them. Next is the Student Placement Summary reproducible sheet that can assist with tracking the placement of each student based on his or her test results. Finally, there are Recording Forms for each of the seven placement tests followed by the Word Sets for Levels 1-7.

Caught Reading offers two types of placement exams to give teachers flexibility in testing and placing students in the appropriate instructional level. The *Teacher's Manual* includes one-page placement tests, each including a high-frequency word recognition quiz, to help teachers quickly and accurately place students. In the *Assessment Manual*, longer placement tests provide more comprehensive data about each student's instructional needs, by posing a variety of multiple-choice and short-answer questions.

Additional diagnostic tests, such as the Elementary Spelling Inventory and the Names Test of Decoding, supplement placement data by indicating which words and sounds students struggle with the most. An Interest Inventory further helps teachers identify students' interests and aspirations in reading, in order to better prepare lessons.

Caught Reading

Description

No evaluation instrument can take the place of your own judgment. However, you may wish to supplement your judgment with tools such as the *Caught Reading* Placement Tests. These placement tests are designed to guide you in placing your students in the *Caught Reading* program. Each test is easy to administer and should be given one-on-one to individual students. You may begin the testing at any of the seven levels, depending on your initial estimation of a student's reading level, or you may choose to begin the testing with the Level 1 Test.

Each test has two parts. Part A is designed to indicate how well a student reads and recognizes words in isolation, both decodable and sight words. The words are high-utility and representative of the text found in a particular level of *Caught Reading*. Part B tests listening and reading comprehension on both recall and inferential levels. The passage in Part B should be read aloud to the student. This combination of word recognition and listening comprehension is the best indicator for accurate placement in *Caught Reading*.

Administration and Scoring

Make copies of one Individual Recording Form set (Tests 1–7) and one Student Placement Summary for each student. You may also choose to photocopy the Word Sets found on page xxix or, if you prefer, have students read the Word Sets directly from this *Teacher's Manual*. All the Word Sets appear on one page. To accommodate some students, you may need to provide each Word Set separately. Administer the test individually to the student, recording his or her responses on the Recording Form.

The placement process for *Caught Reading* is simple:

1. Place an X in the box next to any item that is read or answered incorrectly from the Word Set in Part A or the questions following the listening comprehension passage in Part B.

2. Transfer the information from the Individual Recording Form to the Student Placement Summary.

3. If the student scores no more than three incorrect words in Part A and no more than one incorrect answer in Part B, progress to the next level test.

4. Continue testing until the student has more than seven boxes marked X in Part A and more than one box marked X in Part B on any one test.

5. Place the student at the appropriate level in *Caught Reading*. (Special conditions in Test 1 may indicate that the student should be placed in *Getting Ready*.) At the bottom of each individual test, there is a Summary that will give you additional information to aid you in placement.

Remember that the *Caught Reading* Placement Tests are designed to supplement your own estimation and judgment—not replace it.

Caught Reading

Name: _____ Date: _____

LEVEL 1 TEST	NOTES
PART A: INCORRECT RESPONSES _____	
PART B: INCORRECT RESPONSES _____	

LEVEL 2 TEST	NOTES
PART A: INCORRECT RESPONSES _____	
PART B: INCORRECT RESPONSES _____	

LEVEL 3 TEST	NOTES
PART A: INCORRECT RESPONSES _____	
PART B: INCORRECT RESPONSES _____	

LEVEL 4 TEST	NOTES
PART A: INCORRECT RESPONSES _____	
PART B: INCORRECT RESPONSES _____	

LEVEL 5 TEST	NOTES
PART A: INCORRECT RESPONSES _____	
PART B: INCORRECT RESPONSES _____	

LEVEL 6 TEST	NOTES
PART A: INCORRECT RESPONSES _____	
PART B: INCORRECT RESPONSES _____	

LEVEL 7 TEST	NOTES
PART A: INCORRECT RESPONSES _____	
PART B: INCORRECT RESPONSES _____	

PLACEMENT: *CAUGHT READING LEVEL* _____

Caught Reading

Name: _____ Date: _____

Ask the student to read the words from Word Set 1. If the student is unsure of the word, encourage him or her to guess. Place an X in the box next to each word the student cannot read or mispronounces.

PART A (WORD SET 1)

☐ job	☐ play	☐ want	☐ he	☐ am
☐ dog	☐ get	☐ walk	☐ game	☐ is
☐ say	☐ go	☐ what	☐ off	☐ you
☐ think	☐ make	☐ like	☐ me	☐ but

PART B

Tell the student you are going to read a passage one time only, and then ask him or her several questions. Read the passage, ask the questions, and place an X in the box beside any question that the student fails to answer or answers incorrectly.

Joel and his sister Beth went to California to visit their grandma. It had been almost a year since Joel and Beth had seen Grandma, and they were looking forward to all the fun they knew they would have. They liked to collect shells on the beach, drive through the mountains, look at the family photo albums, play board games, and listen to Grandma sing and play the piano. Joel and Beth plan to go back home to North Carolina in three weeks.

☐ **1.** Where do Joel and Beth live? (*Response should indicate North Carolina.*)

☐ **2.** Name two things Joel and Beth like to do when they visit their grandmother. (*Student should name any two of the following: collect shells, drive through the mountains, look at family photo albums, play board games, listen to Grandma sing and play the piano.*)

☐ **3.** How do Joel and Beth feel about their grandmother? (*Response should indicate that they enjoy being around her or they like spending time with her.*)

TEST 1 SUMMARY	• If the student scored no more than three incorrect in Part A and no more than one incorrect in Part B, administer Test 2.
PART A: INCORRECT RESPONSES _____	• If the student scored no more than seven incorrect in Part A and no more than two incorrect in Part B, place the student in *Caught Reading* Worktext 1.
PART B: INCORRECT RESPONSES _____	• If the student scored more than seven incorrect in Part A and more than two incorrect in Part B, place the student in *Caught Reading, Getting Ready*.

Caught Reading

Name: _____ Date: _____

Ask the student to read the words from Word Set 2. If the student is unsure of the word, encourage him or her to guess. Place an X in the box next to each word the student cannot read or mispronounces.

PART A (WORD SET 2)

☐ will	☐ snow	☐ feeling	☐ ideas	☐ gives
☐ because	☐ after	☐ know	☐ look	☐ they
☐ principal	☐ raise	☐ believe	☐ our	☐ ever
☐ seen	☐ really	☐ start	☐ it's	☐ this

PART B

Tell the student you are going to read a passage one time only, and then ask him or her several questions. Read the passage, ask the questions, and place an X in the box beside any question that the student fails to answer or answers incorrectly.

Four students from Central City High School decided to organize a clean-up at the local park. They talked with other students at school, decided on the second Saturday in March for the clean-up day, made signs advertising the project, and asked local businesses for their help. Fifty-five students volunteered to help and several businesses gladly donated trash bags, rakes, brooms, and even refreshments for the volunteers.

By the second Saturday in March, everyone was ready. The clean-up day was a big success. The citizens in town got a sparkling-clean park, and the students had a good time working with each other. The *Central City News* did a front-page story on the project and the four proud students who had organized this gift to Central City.

☐ **1.** How many students volunteered to work with the original organizers of the clean-up project? (*55*)

☐ **2.** Why did the *Central City News* write a story about the clean-up project? (*Response should indicate the student's understanding of a newsworthy community-service event.*)

☐ **3.** Why did the business people donate materials and refreshments for the clean-up? (*Response should indicate that the businesses were as concerned about the park's clean-up as the students or that the businesses felt that they were a part of a concerned community.*)

TEST 2 SUMMARY	
PART A: INCORRECT RESPONSES _____	• If the student scored no more than three incorrect in Part A and no more than one incorrect in Part B, administer Test 3.
PART B: INCORRECT RESPONSES _____	• If the student scored no more than seven incorrect in Part A and no more than two incorrect in Part B, place the student in *Caught Reading* Worktext 2.

Caught Reading

Name: _____ Date: _____

Ask the student to read the words from Word Set 3. If the student is unsure of the word, encourage him or her to guess. Place an X in the box next to each word the student cannot read or mispronounces.

PART A (WORD SET 3)

☐ below	☐ apart	☐ along	☐ thing	☐ old
☐ right	☐ together	☐ answer	☐ describe	☐ box
☐ change	☐ yes	☐ done	☐ gone	☐ turn
☐ read	☐ room	☐ from	☐ each	☐ had

PART B

Tell the student you are going to read a passage one time only, and then ask him or her several questions. Read the passage, ask the questions, and place an X in the box beside any question that the student fails to answer or answers incorrectly.

Nicholas and his father had been planning a camping trip for two months. They had been camping many times before, but this was the first time they were going camping in another state. It would be a four-hour drive to Oregon, but they both thought it would be worth it. They had written to the Oregon Park Service for information about camping sites and had gotten information about several sites they thought would be good ones.

Nicholas and his dad had a lot of camping gear, but they needed just a few new things: a camp stove, a new liner for the inside floor of their tent, two compasses for hiking, and a cooler. They were excited and ready for their camping trip.

☐ **1.** How do you know this isn't Nicholas and his father's first camping trip? (*The passage says they've gone camping many times before.*)

☐ **2.** What is one camping item that Nicholas and his father probably have already? (*Since they were buying a new liner for their tent, the answer should include "tent." However, you may accept any other reasonable piece of camping gear other than a camp stove, compasses, or cooler.*)

☐ **3.** How do you know that Nicholas and his father don't live in Oregon? (*Oregon was a four-hour out-of-state trip for them.*)

TEST 3 SUMMARY	
PART A: INCORRECT RESPONSES _____	• If the student scored no more than three incorrect in Part A and no more than one incorrect in Part B, administer Test 4.
PART B: INCORRECT RESPONSES _____	• If the student scored no more than seven incorrect in Part A and no more than two incorrect in Part B, place the student in *Caught Reading* Worktext 3.

Caught Reading

Name: _____ Date: _____

Ask the student to read the words from Word Set 4. If the student is unsure of the word, encourage him or her to guess. Place an X in the box next to each word the student cannot read or mispronounces.

PART A (WORD SET 4)

☐ still	☐ different	☐ kind	☐ water	☐ radio
☐ never	☐ animal	☐ remember	☐ living	☐ tried
☐ earth	☐ against	☐ enough	☐ between	☐ isn't
☐ space	☐ between	☐ anywhere	☐ enough	☐ those

PART B

Tell the student you are going to read a passage one time only, and then ask him or her several questions. Read the passage, ask the questions, and place an X in the box beside any question that the student fails to answer or answers incorrectly.

I collect things—all kinds of things. For example, I collect shoestrings with advertising on them. I have one set that advertises a computer, one that advertises sunglasses, and another that is an ad for a pro-football team. I have managed to collect 35 sets of shoestrings with ads on them. I also collect baseball and basketball cards, old keys, small wooden boxes, old-time bottle caps, and guitar picks. You'd think my room in our apartment would be a real mess, but it's not, because all my collections are organized in my small wooden boxes.

My mom used to think that my collections were just junk until last week. On Wednesday, she broke a shoestring on one of her running shoes. My collection came to the rescue and she was able to meet her running partner on time. On Saturday, she bought an old chest that she thinks is an antique at a yard sale. One of the drawers was locked. Once again my collection came to the rescue. One of my old skeleton keys opened the locked drawer just like it was made for it. Mom told me that we probably would be in a real fix without my collection. She even sat down with me on Sunday and looked at all my stuff. Now she calls me "The Collector King." I like that.

☐ **1.** Where does the writer live? (*an apartment*)

☐ **2.** Name three things that the writer likes to collect. (*Student should name any three of the following: shoestrings, baseball/basketball cards, old keys, small wooden boxes, old-time bottle caps, guitar picks.*)

☐ **3.** Why did the writer's mom change her mind about the collection? (*Response should indicate that parts of the collection became useful.*)

TEST 4 SUMMARY	• If the student scored no more than three incorrect in Part A and no more than one incorrect in Part B, administer Test 5.
PART A: INCORRECT RESPONSES _____ **PART B: INCORRECT RESPONSES** _____	• If the student scored no more than seven incorrect in Part A and no more than two incorrect in Part B, place the student in *Caught Reading* Worktext 4.

Caught Reading

Name: _____ Date: _____

Ask the student to read the words from Word Set 5. If the student is unsure of the word, encourage him or her to guess. Place an X in the box next to each word the student cannot read or mispronounces.

PART A (WORD SET 5)

☐ test ☐ politics ☐ farm ☐ learn ☐ pants

☐ history ☐ strong ☐ born ☐ town ☐ ready

☐ finish ☐ strike ☐ city ☐ summer ☐ thought

☐ listen ☐ yourself ☐ police ☐ neighbor ☐ found

PART B

Tell the student you are going to read a passage one time only, and then ask him or her several questions. Read the passage, ask the questions, and place an X in the box beside any question that the student fails to answer or answers incorrectly.

It wasn't often that the "Bad Rock" band made it to Ohio, and Chris and T.J. had tickets. The seats were pretty high up in the stadium, but at least they were in. The night before the concert, Chris's little sister lost Murphy, her cat. Chris located the cat stuck in a tree. Against his better judgment, Chris climbed the tree to rescue Murphy, but he slipped and fell to the ground.

At the hospital emergency room, Chris learned he had broken both legs and would be in a wheelchair for at least six weeks. As he was waiting for the emergency room technician to bring him a wheelchair, he began talking to a guy sitting next to him in the waiting room. The guy's name was Jake, and he had slipped on some steps and broken his left leg and his right ankle. He was also waiting for a wheelchair.

Chris told Jake how unhappy he was—not just because he'd broken his legs—but also because he'd miss the "Bad Rock" concert. Chris was pretty sure he couldn't get his wheelchair up all those stairs at the stadium. Jake told Chris that he was going to be at the concert, too. He offered to give Chris special tickets that would let Chris and T.J. sit in a place where wheelchairs were allowed. Jake would even have the tickets brought to Chris's house the next morning. Chris thanked Jake.

The next night at the concert, Chris and T.J. were sitting in the front row—Chris in his wheelchair, and T.J. in his seat—when "Bad Rock" came onstage. Imagine Chris's surprise when Jake played his guitar from his wheelchair with a big wink at Chris in the front row!

☐ **1.** Where do Chris and T.J. live? (*Ohio*)

☐ **2.** How did Chris meet Jake? (*Both had broken bones and were in the hospital waiting room together, so they began to talk.*)

☐ **3.** How do you think Chris felt about seeing Jake on stage? (*Answers should indicate student's understanding that he was surprised and pleased.*)

TEST 5 SUMMARY	
PART A: INCORRECT RESPONSES _____	• If the student scored no more than three incorrect in Part A and no more than one incorrect in Part B, administer Test 6.
PART B: INCORRECT RESPONSES _____	• If the student scored no more than seven incorrect in Part A and no more than two incorrect in Part B, place the student in *Caught Reading* Worktext 5.

Caught Reading

Name: _____ Date: _____

Ask the student to read the words from Word Set 6. If the student is unsure of the word, encourage him or her to guess. Place an X in the box next to each word the student cannot read or mispronounces.

PART A (WORD SET 6)

☐ begin	☐ which	☐ alone	☐ music	☐ street
☐ ride	☐ feet	☐ paper	☐ very	☐ since
☐ telephone	☐ country	☐ across	☐ trouble	☐ might
☐ restaurant	☐ suddenly	☐ storm	☐ slow	☐ won't

PART B

Tell the student you are going to read a passage one time only, and then ask him or her several questions. Read the passage, ask the questions, and place an X in the box beside any question that the student fails to answer or answers incorrectly.

Kate hated the idea of moving to a new city. She and her mom had moved four times in the last three years, and Kate thought that was three times too many. She liked the kids she met in each place—especially here in Thomas Falls, and especially her best friend Toni—but it was increasingly harder to make friends when she felt like she'd be leaving them almost as soon as she'd met them.

"Today is my last day at school here," Kate said to her friend Toni. "I wish I wasn't moving away. We've just gotten to be friends, and it's so hard to find good friends."

"I know what you mean," Toni replied. "I'm going to miss you a lot. There's no one else who is as patient as you are. I think I would have flunked history if you hadn't helped me study. Where are you going to live, Kate?"

"We're moving to a horrible place. I don't know anyone, and I don't even want to know anyone," said Kate. "It's called Singer City, and I know I'm going to hate it!"

Toni laughed and said, "Oh, I don't think it's going to be so bad. It's got a terrific game center, a good basketball team, and some really cool kids. And besides, there'll be a friend of yours there who you can see every other weekend," she continued.

"What are you talking about?" asked Kate. "I told you I don't know anybody there, and I don't want to know anybody."

"Yes," said Toni. "But I'll bet you didn't know my dad is moving there, and I'll be visiting him every other weekend."

"Well . . . maybe Singer City won't be that bad," chuckled Kate. "Not that bad at all."

☐ **1.** Who is Kate's best friend in Thomas Falls? (*Toni*)

☐ **2.** Why doesn't Kate want to make any friends in Singer City? (*Responses should indicate an understanding of Kate's feeling that as soon as she makes friends, she feels she has to leave them.*)

☐ **3.** What do you predict will happen to Kate when she moves to Singer City? (*Answers will vary but should indicate student's understanding that Kate will make new friends, but still keep Toni as a friend and see her every other weekend.*)

TEST 6 SUMMARY	• If the student scored no more than three incorrect in Part A and no more than one incorrect in Part B, administer Test 7.
PART A: INCORRECT RESPONSES _____	
PART B: INCORRECT RESPONSES _____	• If the student scored no more than seven incorrect in Part A and no more than two incorrect in Part B, place the student in *Caught Reading* Worktext 6.

Caught Reading

Name: _____ Date: _____

Ask the student to read the words from Word Set 7. If the student is unsure of the word, encourage him or her to guess. Place an X in the box next to each word a student cannot read or mispronounces.

PART A (WORD SET 7)

☐ almost	☐ important	☐ bring	☐ business	☐ movie
☐ yesterday	☐ newspaper	☐ engine	☐ brother	☐ store
☐ company	☐ parents	☐ crowd	☐ practice	☐ chance
☐ special	☐ correct	☐ price	☐ person	☐ empty

PART B

Tell the student you are going to read a passage one time only, and then ask him or her several questions. Read the passage, ask the questions, and place an X in the box beside any question that the student fails to answer or answers incorrectly.

Jeff was furious that he had to spend his summer on the farm with his Uncle Max. His mom had started a new job, and she had to leave town for some special training for two whole months. Jeff knew he was a responsible person, but his mom didn't think he was old enough to live on his own for two months. So, here he was—stuck on a farm in the middle of nowhere with nothing to do, and no one to do it with. Uncle Max was an OK guy, but he was too busy taking care of his horses to spend any time with Jeff, and Jeff had no interest in horses. Jeff felt almost like an orphan.

Jeff looked up as Uncle Max came in the door wearing a worried look. "I don't know what's wrong with the mare in the barn. She's pretty sick, and I don't know if she can deliver the foal. I may need some help from you, Jeff."

Jeff was not thrilled, but he didn't know how to turn Uncle Max down, so he said, "Sure."

They both made their way to the barn, where the golden mare was, as Uncle Max had said, in pain and clearly having problems. Uncle Max took control, and Jeff did everything Uncle Max directed. In the end, though, the mare gave up the fight and died.

"Quick," said Uncle Max. "Let's get the foal." So he and Jeff worked together, and soon there was a beautiful gray-colored foal. "You rub the foal with these towels," said Uncle Max, "while I go get a bottle and some milk to feed him."

Jeff looked into the foal's frightened eyes as he rubbed and dried. "I know how you feel, little one," Jeff said to the foal in a low and comforting voice. "I'm not a real orphan like you, but I know how you feel."

Uncle Max soon came back with a bottle that he gave to Jeff to feed to the foal. The foal nuzzled the bottle and began to drink with loud slurps. Jeff held the bottle until the foal was finished, and then he hugged the newborn. "I think you need me, little one. And I'm going to be here to help you," Jeff whispered to the foal. Suddenly, the summer didn't seem so bad after all.

☐ **1.** Why did Jeff have to spend the summer with Uncle Max? (*His mom had a new job and had to go to special training for two months, and she didn't want Jeff to be alone.*)

☐ **2.** What is the name for a newborn horse? (*foal*)

☐ **3.** Why do you think Jeff changed his mind about the summer at Uncle Max's? (*Answers will vary but should indicate student's understanding that Jeff felt needed and felt responsible for the foal.*)

TEST 7 SUMMARY	• If the student scored no more than seven incorrect in Part A and no more than two incorrect in Part B, place the student in *Caught Reading* Worktext 7.
PART A: INCORRECT RESPONSES _____	
PART B: INCORRECT RESPONSES _____	

Caught Reading

Name: _____ Date: _____

WORD SET 1

1. job	5. play	9. want	13. he	17. am
2. dog	6. get	10. walk	14. game	18. is
3. say	7. go	11. what	15. off	19. you
4. think	8. make	12. like	16. me	20. but

WORD SET 2

1. will	5. snow	9. feeling	13. ideas	17. gives
2. because	6. after	10. know	14. look	18. they
3. principal	7. raise	11. believe	15. our	19. ever
4. seen	8. really	12. start	16. it's	20. this

WORD SET 3

1. below	5. apart	9. along	13. thing	17. old
2. right	6. together	10. answer	14. describe	18. box
3. change	7. yes	11. done	15. gone	19. turn
4. read	8. room	12. from	16. each	20. had

WORD SET 4

1. still	5. different	9. kind	13. water	17. radio
2. never	6. animal	10. remember	14. living	18. tried
3. earth	7. against	11. enough	15. between	19. isn't
4. space	8. between	12. anywhere	16. enough	20. those

WORD SET 5

1. test	5. politics	9. farm	13. learn	17. pants
2. history	6. strong	10. born	14. town	18. ready
3. finish	7. strike	11. city	15. summer	19. thought
4. listen	8. yourself	12. police	16. neighbor	20. found

WORD SET 6

1. begin	5. which	9. alone	13. music	17. street
2. ride	6. feet	10. paper	14. very	18. since
3. telephone	7. country	11. across	15. trouble	19. might
4. restaurant	8. suddenly	12. storm	16. slow	20. won't

WORD SET 7

1. almost	5. important	9. bring	13. business	17. movie
2. yesterday	6. newspaper	10. engine	14. brother	18. store
3. company	7. parents	11. crowd	15. practice	19. chance
4. special	8. correct	12. price	16. person	20. empty

OBJECTIVES

Phonemic Awareness

• Recognize sounds made by short vowels, long vowels, and consonants

• Discriminate sounds in the initial, final, and medial positions of words

• Develop phonemic awareness while decoding words with prefixes and suffixes, compound words, and multisyllabic words

Phonics

• Recognize that letters represent vowel and consonant sounds

• Match consonant letters to sounds, including consonants that make two sounds (*c* and *g*)

• Recognize that the consonant digraphs, double consonants, and other consonant pairs such as *ch, sh, th, wh, ff, ll, ss, ck, wr, gn, ng*, and *mb* make only one sound

• Identify and match long-, short-, and *r*-controlled vowel sounds to letters

Word Identification

• Decode and read words with three to six phonemes

• Distinguish short- and long-vowel patterns in words

• Identify words containing hard or soft consonant sounds, consonant blends, and single sounds for more than one letter

• Recognize that some base words do not change when prefixes or suffixes are added

Reading

• Apply decoding skills by reading a variety of texts, including texts that include long-vowel, compound, two-syllable, and multisyllabic words

• Read passages and fill in missing words

Writing

• Apply writing skills by writing a variety of short passages including a poem, sports cheer, ad, and invitation

• Write sentences that sequence the order of events

• Write lists of rhyming words

Speaking and Listening

• Apply decoding skills and phonemic awareness by reading aloud nonsense words, tongue-twisters, and poems

Note: Most of the instructional material in the Worktext at this level is beyond the reading level of the student. Therefore, teachers will need to provide appropriate levels of support as the student works through the materials.

CHAPTER 1
Tools for *Getting Ready*

LESSON 1

OBJECTIVES
- Students will recognize that the upper and lower case letters of the alphabet represent vowel sounds and consonants
- Students will match consonant sounds to corresponding letters
- Students will identify consonants that can make two sounds

WORD BANK OF WORDS
CONTAINING *c, g, s, x*

pencil	game	nose	xylophone
cake	garage	serious	Xerox
coffee	dragon	please	fax
circle	gentle	sit	box
cycle	gauge	sock	six

MATERIALS
Worktext, page 5
Teacher's Manual, pages 1–2
Letter cards from A to Z

Teacher Tip

It may be surprising to find that some students may not have complete phonics or alphabetic knowledge. They may not have correctly associated specific letters to sounds. Before moving into Chapter 2, which focuses on three-sound words, it will be important for students to have a basic knowledge of the alphabet and the sounds each letter or combinations of letters make. You may wish to use this chapter as a reference tool while your students work through Chapters 2–7.

▶ THE ALPHABET
Sounds and Letters, From A to Z

- Provide each student with a shuffled set of letter cards, from A to Z. Ask them to organize the cards in alphabetical order.
- As you see each student complete the task, ask the student to point to each letter card, beginning with A, and name the letter. Make a checklist to keep track of students who don't have complete alphabetic knowledge and need additional work with specific sounds and letters.

Categories, From A to Z

- Make columns of words for each letter of the alphabet. Invite students to put their first names under the correct category, such as *Mm* for *Maya*, or *Jj* for *Joseph*. Have them complete the same routine with their last names, such as *Oo* for *Ortiz*. Rotating around the room, ask students to add their favorite words under the correct category.
- Brainstorm these words by encouraging students to think of their favorite sports, activities, and foods. Have them also look around the room and find objects in the room that they can add to the columns. As students progress through *Getting Ready*, have them continue adding words they've decoded and can read.

▶ CONSONANTS
One-Sound Consonants

Distribute photocopies of the alphabet. Tell students that you want to focus on the consonants first. Invite students to circle all of the consonants in the alphabet. Explain that most consonants make one sound, but some can make two sounds, such as *c*, *g*, *s*, and *x*. Save those consonants for later and begin by having students name the others and say each sound.

Teacher Tip

As students say the sound that each letter makes, coach them to say each sound without an *uh* at the end of it. For example, *Bb* is /*b*/, not *buh*. *Zz* is *zzzzz*, not *zuh*. The stop consonants such as /*b*/ or /*d*/ will be more difficult to say without the *uh*. Encourage students to say them as short as possible. By not adding a vowel sound at the end, students will be less confused when they begin segmenting and decoding three-sound words, such as *bit*. Instead of /*bu*/ /*i*/ /*tuh*/, they will segment and decode it correctly: /*b*/ /*i*/ /*t*/.

Alliterative Tongue Twisters

- Working with consonants that make one sound, have students brainstorm funny tongue twisters, such as *Dan Dougherty drives a Dodge to Dartmouth, eating donuts with Dalia Darling and her dogs, Diggy and Dougie.*
- Encourage students to use the dictionary to create their tongue twisters.

Two-Sound Consonants

- Write the following categories on the board:

Cc		Gg		Ss		Xx	
/k/	/s/	/g/	/j/	/s/	/z/	/ks/	/z/

  Mention to students that some consonants make more than one sound. Begin working with words in the Word Bank that contain the letter *c*. Since students may not be able to decode the words, point to the following words and say each one, having students echo you: **pencil**, **cake**, **coffee**, **circle**, **cycle**. Next, invite students to put each word under the correct category. Explain that some of the words have a hard sound like /k/, while other words have a soft sound, like /s/. Ask them if any words contain both sounds. (*circle, cycle*)

- Now have students work with hard and soft *g*, repeating the same routine with words from the Word Bank. In Chapter 4, students will be completing spelling exercises on both hard and soft *c* and *g*. (Worktext pages 25–26)

- Complete the other categories on the board for *s* and *x*, using words from the Word Bank.

▶ PRACTICE

Favorite Words

Have students complete Worktext page 5, having them associate and list a favorite word for each letter of the alphabet.

Favorite Words

Draw a circle around each vowel. Draw a square around each consonant. Below each letter of the alphabet, write a favorite word that begins with that letter. If you can't think of a word, you can use the dictionary for help.

a	b	c
d	e	f
g	h	i
j	k	l
m	n	o
p	q	r
s	t	u
v	w	x
y	z	

Lesson 1 • 5

Worktext page 5

LESSON 2

OBJECTIVES

- Students will recognize that consonant digraphs such as *ch*, *sh*, *th*, and *wh* represent one sound
- Students will identify words containing consonant digraphs

WORD BANK OF WORDS CONTAINING CONSONANT DIGRAPHS

sheep	chill	thing	white
shake	cheer	thick	wheat
shy	chop	think	whale
shed	cheese	that	while
shin	chat	then	when

MATERIALS

Worktext, page 6
Teacher's Manual, page 3
Letter cards and consonant digraph cards, *ch*, *sh*, *th*, *wh*

▶ **CONSONANT DIGRAPHS**

Sorting Sounds

Write the following categories on the board: **ch**, **sh**, **th**, and **wh**. Point to and say each sound, having students echo you. Then say the word **sheep**, elongating and stretching the initial consonant digraph. Ask a volunteer to name the category it belongs to, writing the word underneath it. Do the same routine with the words *chill*, *thing*, and *white*.

Rhyming Sounds

Say the word **hill**. Ask students to think of a word that rhymes with *hill* and begins with *ch*. (*chill*) Then write the word under that category. Do the same routine with the following words: *bake/shake*; *pop/chop*; *pick/thick*; and *bite/white*.

▶ **PRACTICE**

Word Search

Have students turn to page 6 in the Worktext. Have them find hidden words on the Word Search board and circle them. Then ask them to sort the words according to each initial consonant digraph.

LESSON 2

Word Search
On the Word Search board, locate and circle words that begin with *ch*, *sh*, *th*, and *wh*. The words can go down, across, diagonally, or backward. When you find each word, you can cross it out in the Word Bank.

WORD BANK

sheep	chill	thing	white
cheer	thick	wheat	shake
whale	think	chop	shy
that	while	shed	cheese
when	shin	chat	then

J	L	T	S	E	F	K	W	I	T	W
R	Z	H	H	G	C	W	H	U	H	H
C	H	E	E	R	S	H	E	D	I	A
H	B	N	E	J	Q	E	A	W	N	L
E	V	G	P	Q	E	N	T	T	K	E
E	T	J	N	Q	T	H	I	C	K	J
S	A	L	B	I	I	S	V	P	R	N
E	H	K	H	S	H	A	K	E	I	X
R	T	Y	S	M	W	T	C	H	O	P
C	H	I	L	L	V	J	S	D	D	Y
F	T	K	J	H	B	W	H	I	L	E

6 • Chapter 1

Worktext page 6

LESSON 3

OBJECTIVES
- Students will recognize that long vowels make the same sound as their letter name
- Students will identify long-vowel words with the spelling pattern vowel-consonant-*e*, as well as vowel pairs *ai*, *ay*, *ee*, *ea*, *ie*, *oa*, and *ow*

WORD BANK OF LONG-VOWEL WORDS

game	need	bike	cove	tune
main	deep	tie	row	mule
day	meal	kite	boat	June
rain	each	pie	soap	cute

MATERIALS
Worktext, page 7
Teacher's Manual, page 4
Letter cards

▶ LONG VOWELS

Distribute photocopies of the alphabet. Ask students to circle the letters that represent vowel sounds. Mention to students that long vowels make the same sound as their letter names. For example, long *a* sounds like /*a*/ in *ate*; long *e* sounds like /*e*/ in *eat*; long *i* sounds like /*i*/ in *ice*; long *o* sounds like /*o*/ in *open*; and long *u* sounds like /*u*/ in *uniform*.

Sorting Sounds

Write the following categories on the board: **long a**, **long e**, **long i**, **long o**, and **long u**. Explain to students that long-vowel words can be spelled vowel-consonant-*e*, as in *bake*, *Pete*, *hike*, *hope*, and *cube*. Write the words under the correct categories. Mention that in a vowel pair where two vowels are next to each other, the first vowel says its name, while the second one is silent, as in *stain*, *lie*, *reach*, and *coat*. Also explain that *ay*, when it is at the end of a word, usually sounds like long *a*, as in *hay*. Add these words to the categories. Coach students in brainstorming words that contain long vowels, and have volunteers sound out and write these words on the board.

Rhyming Sounds

Provide a set of letter cards to pairs of students. Have them build the word *game*. Then ask them to make the word *came*, substituting the initial consonant to form a new long *a* word. Then ask them to make the words *fame*, *name*, *same*, and *tame*. Use other words in the Word Bank to have students build other long-vowel and rhyming words.

▶ PRACTICE

Fill in the Blanks

Have students turn to page 7 in their Worktexts. Using their Word Bank as a reference, have them fill in the blanks to create long-vowel words. You may wish to have students work in pairs for this activity. Rotating around the room, help students decode and read the words. Keep a checklist handy to record whether students are able to sound out a consonant or vowel.

LESSON 3

Fill in the Blanks
Look at each word and fill in the blanks to make long-vowel words.
To help you complete this activity, you can find each word in the
Word Bank. Afterward, take turns reading each word with a partner.

WORD BANK

cute	soap	pie	each	rain
need	bike	cove	tune	game
deep	tie	row	mule	main
boat	June	kite	meal	day

1. g __ m __
2. n __ __ d
3. b __ k __
4. c __ v __
5. t __ n __
6. m __ __ n
7. d __ __ p
8. t __ __
9. r __ w
10. m __ l __

11. d __ __
12. m __ __ l
13. k __ t __
14. b __ __ t
15. J __ n __
16. r __ __ n
17. __ __ c h
18. p __ __
19. s __ __ p
20. c __ t __

Lesson 3 • 7

Worktext page 7